Table of Contents

INTRODUCTION

Almost everyone will have to stand up and talk in public at some stage in their life: perhaps in class or at assembly in school; maybe in a debating event at school or university; or at a ceremonial event like a wedding as best man or woman; or you might be the one giving the eulogy at the funeral of a relative or friend; you may be making an interview pitch to a potential academic tutor or employer; or making a commercial pitch to a potential client; perhaps at an event to give a word of thanks; or as a keynote speaker; or giving a sermon; or introducing a speaker at a conference; perhaps at a party-political gathering; or an acceptance speech after receiving an award; or simply as an after-dinner speaker.

There will be many other such occasions when the spotlight could fall on you. So, it would be helpful to learn how to do it and to master a unique Oratory Aide-Memoire for your speeches that will guarantee success when the big day comes.

This book is unashamedly aimed at the younger generations – those starting out in life – with a view to giving them something that will set them up for whatever the future may hold.

That said, we none of us are too old to learn, so there is probably something in these chapters for all those novices and others who have to stand up in front of others and speak.

Having been a soldier for almost all of my working life I know the value of sound preparation and of well-practised drills and skills. I have come to learn that there are many parallels between preparing for and carrying out a military operation and doing the same for a public speaking event.

Understanding the reason why soldiers do what they do will reinforce the advice I have laid down throughout this book. I also hope it will make it more interesting and help you remember things more easily.

Whether it is your lack of confidence or scarcity of opportunity that prevents you from speaking in public, or whether it is simply that you do not know where to begin, because no one has taught you how to master this invaluable skill, the fog will be lifted as you progress through these chapters.

If you take on board what I have to say, you will certainly be able to speak in front of an audience with increased confidence. Your ability to do so will grow on reading it and continue to develop thereafter.

You will soon feel that it is one of the best investments you have ever made. Effective public speaking skills will certainly help you in your career. They go hand in hand with leadership abilities, critical thinking and professionalism. They are also a very good way to build your credibility.

Moreover, if you speak well in public, it is certainly a great asset when it comes to getting a job and getting promoted thereafter.

There are any number of books on the market that cover the art of public speaking, and some of them are very good. But, you will find it difficult to source a book that covers both the art and the science that will help you to become proficient at this essential skill. None has my unique aide-memoire.

Step by step, I will take you through the processes and procedures that will allow you to prepare yourself for and carry out a successful public speaking engagement, however big or small that might be.

I won't baffle you with the sort of information that a neuroscientist or a behavioural scientist would likely give you. Mine is pure, practical advice.

If you want something that borders on being a personal guide, as well as an influential work on speaking in public, you need go no further.

Everything you need is here; even a couple of pages at the back for jotting down your notes as you read it through.

That is not to say that you will become a Churchill overnight. Even he took a number of years to perfect what we now regard as a unique manner in getting his messages across. But, you will certainly be equipped to construct and deliver a short and convincing talk, if you follow the guidance I am giving.

As you start out on your public speaking journey, try to find an engagement that puts you among friends and allows you to talk on something that you understand well. There's nothing like a resounding success to give you the confidence to go on to bigger and more testing engagements.

You might well be asking yourself why you should be listening to me. There will, of course, be others whose qualifications will be better than mine, and some will have given a larger number of speeches in their time.

But, few, if any, will have had a full Army career, which had me regularly standing in front of numerous and varying audiences, big and small, at home and overseas, and delivering important messages to them; sometimes at critical times.

I have had the opportunity to reflect on how well or not I came across and to work out why. This book is a fusion of the lessons I learned over my lifetime and am happy to pass on to new generations.

People often ask me if there is such a thing as a born orator, and I always give the same answer that I do to a similar question about born leaders. I firmly believe in the analogy that we are all born with a pack of cards: we are all good at some things and some of us are better than others at certain things. So, whereas you might be a 3 of Clubs at playing the violin, you might be a King of Diamonds at playing football.

The chances are that you will have noticed that there are many things you do that rate in the lower card numbers, but there are a couple of things that you inherently possess that are up there in the Queens and Kings.

Most importantly, I also believe that we can all self-develop or be developed, to improve our hand of cards. We just need someone to help pull it out of us.

You would not be reading this book if you did not agree. I wish you luck on your journey to becoming an Ace of Hearts at public speaking.

PART I

PLANNING & PREPARATION

CHAPTER 1 – ANALYSIS

The Seven Ps

All soldiers will know what I mean when I mention the Seven Ps. It gets drilled into them from the moment they arrive at their initial training establishment.

Almost the first thing their instructor tells them is: '*Prior Planning and Preparation Prevents Pathetically Poor Performance*' (although I have substituted Pathetically for the shorter, four-letter word more fancied by soldiers).

And so it is with public speaking. If you want your talk, address, speech, interview or pitch to go well, you are going to have to do the legwork beforehand.

There are relatively few people capable of winging it well, unless it is a very short and simple speech. Novices would be wise not to try.

For those of you setting out on this journey, I can do no better than to urge you to adhere to the Seven Ps and do your planning and preparation as a matter of course.

Seasoned painters and decorators will tell you that it's three quarters preparation and one quarter finish. Public speaking should have an even wider balance, with a great deal more time being spent planning and preparing than actually giving the speech. Some believe they need one hour's preparation for each minute of the speech.

Whatever their task, military commanders at all levels begin with a systematic analysis of what is being asked of them; without fail. It includes considering all the factors that impinge on their activity, constraining or otherwise, and leads them to coming up with a number of options for how they might achieve their goal, having taken those factors into account.

The analysis always ends up with the selection of the best option and an outline plan for carrying it out.

So, you, too, need to begin with your analysis. It starts with your mission.

Mission

Military operations, big or small, all have a mission. You might prefer to call this a purpose, a task or a goal but, whatever your terminology, it is the very first thing you need to address.

Quite often you will be fortunate and be given the heading of what you are being asked to talk about. At other times it will be obvious – at a wedding or a funeral, for example.

If you are not told what it is you are to speak on, then that job falls to you to ask whoever is asking you to speak, or to work it out yourself.

It is absolutely critical that the number one thing you write down is your mission, so make sure you have an answer to the all-important question: 'Why am I making this speech?'.

It is something you will be referring back to on a number of occasions in the build-up to your talk, and it influences all the other preparations you make.

I really do mean it when I say you should write it down, as you will see when you get to Part III and learn about the Oratory Aide-Memoire.

Whereas a soldier might find his mission is along the lines of 'To destroy the enemy on Hill 157', it could also be, 'To defeat or to surround or to cut off or to mask the enemy on Hill 157'. The differing verbs are, of course, very important and have a major impact on what will eventually become the plan.

Fortunately, public speaking does not usually come with such dramatic aims. It is likely that your talk will fall into one or other of these categories: to inform; to inspire; to motivate; to educate; to console; to persuade; to entertain; or to sell.

You can probably think of others, but the principle is obvious – be clear from the outset what you are going to talk about, and why.

Most importantly, you will be keen to win over your audience to you and your beliefs, so make sure that you are enthusiastic, if not passionate, about your subject.

Some people will come to listen to you because they are interested in what you are going to talk about. Others will come to see how you put across your subject matter. But, the vast majority will be interested in why it is you are speaking on that subject – the heart of the matter.

Constraints

Next, you need to consider whether or not there are any constraints being placed upon you.

They are, of course, factors you need to consider, but they are special in that they restrict your freedom to do what you want.

For Army missions, the constraints are often to do with the ground or time. Boundaries on the ground may well be given and a time for the operations will often be set, so that coordination of artillery and air support, among other things, can be synchronised.

For public speakers, usually operating on their own, their 'ground' is likely to be the venue in which they are giving their talk. Their time constraints are almost certainly going to be a limit on the length of their talk and a set time to do it. Whatever you do, make sure you know exactly for how long you are expected to speak; this includes any time set aside for questions.

You might, for example, be asked to speak at an evening meal event. The constraint might be that you have to do so either before or after the audience have had their meal (and drink) – two hugely different prospects.

It is in the nature of a constraint that it prevents the speaker from having a free hand in deciding where, when and for how long they are going to talk. Some people, however, will find this strangely liberating; indeed, much needed.

Take on board the constraints, as not to do so will cause you either to run over your time allotted or, worse yet, not turn up at the right place and at the right time.

You can, of course, apply constraints on yourself. One you would have to go a long way to beat is that advocated by Franklin Roosevelt, the US President for 12 years until his death in 1945: *'Be sincere, be brief, be seated.'*

Factors

To keep things simple, you should probably restrict the factors you analyse to those that come under three broad headings: the People, the Place and your Pitch. I know, that's three Ps. If it helps you to remember these groupings of factors, then use it.

The important thing about this part of the analysis is to ensure that, when you consider each factor, you ask yourself the question 'so what?'. For example: my speaking slot is the one straight after lunch – 'so what?' – so, the audience is going to be lethargic and even sleepy. I'll have to make sure I am particularly light and enthusiastic and may have to include more humour than I normally do.

Or, the sound system is notoriously poor at the venue – 'so what?' – so, I will not make the use of videos and I must be prepared to talk more loudly, if the microphone goes down.

Go through every factor systematically, so that you are very clear as to the effect that they might have on your speech.

The People

The enemy is almost invariably the first factor a soldier will consider during his or her analysis.

Unless you are planning to speak at a rival political party's open-air rally, the word 'enemy' will probably not feature on your list.

Indeed, it is imperative that you don't see the people in your audience as the enemy. Hopefully, by the end of your talk they will be among your biggest supporters. That should certainly be your aim and the tenor of your approach – get them on your side and bring them over to your way of thinking.

You need to find out everything you can about those you are going to speak to: their age band; their diversity; the numbers invited; do they know each other; and whether or not they are likely to be onside.

If you can, find out how much your audience is likely to know about your subject matter.

Also gather information, if its available, about how they feel about your views – forewarned is forearmed.

Put simply, it is imperative that you get to know as much as you can about the people who will be sitting in front of you, so that you can construct and pitch your talk to have the best effect.

After all, you have to communicate in the language of your audience.

The Place

It may seem obvious, but where you are giving your speech will have a major influence on how well you go down.

This is the soldiers' 'ground'. He or she will want to study it carefully, know when they are coming into the enemy's view or if they are in 'dead ground'. There is vital ground, high ground, undulating ground, hilly ground and a multiple of others. Ground has such an influence on operations, it is up there close to the enemy in importance.

Similarly, the venue will have a crucial influence on the public speaker.

There are a number of questions to which you need to find the answers. Does the auditorium (if it is one) or the venue have a stage or podium? How big is the seating area? Will the audience be well spread out? Is it well lit? Does it have a stable sound system? Does it have the technical equipment to show videos, or PowerPoint or other media?

Knowing the answers to these questions will help you work out how best to get your messages across and ensure that you are well prepared for the setting. If you blunder in without finding out this information, you will inevitably spend time sorting things out on the day – an unnecessary stress.

You may be giving your pitch in a conference room at the end of the table around which your audience of potential clients are sat. So, you'll be up close and intimate.

If that's the case, your approach will be very different to that for a talk you may be asked to give in the Ondaatje Hall in the Royal Geographical Society, which can seat nearly 500.

The weather will frequently be of major importance to a soldier, but should rarely bother you the public speaker; unless, of course, you are planning to speak at an open-air event, like a sports meeting or a garden party.

However, the time of day and the length of the talk will have some bearing on your analysis. How long do they want you to talk for? Are you on just before or after a meal? Are you the first or last speaker of the day? Do you need to leave time for a question and answer session?

The answers to all these questions will help you judge what the mood of your audience is likely to be and allow you to choose the right content of your talk and the tone in which you will give it.

The Pitch

All of the factors I have mentioned will help to bring you clarity when you come to address the most central of the factors –

those to do with what you are going to say; what I have called the Pitch.

It's worth reflecting, though, that people may be coming to your talk because they are interested in your subject matter or because they are keen to hear you speak, but what will persuade them to accept what you are saying is the reason why you are saying it.

Transmitting your passion or interest in your subject in the most personal and heartfelt manner will always be the difference between a successful and not so successful speech.

All good charitable appeals go to great lengths to explain the 'why'. You only have to watch the BBC's 'Children in Need' appeal to understand the real value of this approach.

At the beginning you analysed your mission, so you should be clear as to what your general subject matter is and what you intend to do, in terms of: to inspire; or to motivate; or to educate etc.

Now it's time to put some meat on the skeleton – your main messages and their supporting messages that you want to get across. This will allow the outline of a plan to start to form in your head.

In an operational analysis, this is where the commander is looking at the tasks he or she is going to have to carry out to achieve the mission. Starting, therefore, to be more specific.

For a speaker, this should not be overly complex, particularly if you know the subject well. But don't move on until you have nailed these messages.

They are your foundation and are rarely something you will wish to change later. Indeed, there will be a number of knock-on effects if you start to change your messages later on, so give yourself enough time to think them through at this stage.

Your aim should be to end up with three nuggets that will form the main part of your talk and all relate very clearly to your main theme. Later, I'll tell you why it is three.

In Part II, I'll go through how you will put those messages together and how you will deliver them.

Options

This is where you take stock of all you have considered in your analysis and think through the different ways open to you to best get your messages across to your audience.

A relatively modest infantry attack on an enemy position might have the options of: left flanking, right flanking or straight up the centre.

For you, the speaker, it may boil down to whether you are going to talk using a handful of slides and videos, or using a flip chart, or simply standing up in front of your audience, unaided, and speaking.

There is a danger that you might decide on this even before you do your analysis. I would caution you against doing so, unless, of course, it is a talk you have given before and already know what works best. Even then, some of the factors (particularly the people) will be different, so you cannot be certain.

Hopefully, as you think through the content of your talk and the arrangements in the venue, you might decide that your audience will be more likely to take in your messages in one particular way.

You should be guided by what you have come to learn about the people who will be in front of you and the surroundings you all find yourselves in.

Look at the advantages and disadvantages of conducting your talk in all the ways possible (the options), and this should lead you to a conclusion – the best option.

Plan

There is absolutely no point in going through this extensive analysis if it doesn't lead you to an outline plan.

In essence, this plan is the structure of your talk, in much the same way as a military plan is the structure of the action they are going to carry out or, to use their term, to execute their mission.

Remember, people will listen to a well-structured talk and be far more attentive than they would be for a rambling, ad hoc speech.

The Rule of Three

Since the time of Aristotle, who wrote about it in his book '*Rhetoric*' some 2,500 years ago, people have been using the Rule of Three technique in their speeches and presentations.

The Rule of Three is based on the fact that people tend to easily remember three things.

It is also a very general principle that ideas presented in threes are inherently more interesting, more enjoyable and more memorable.

Seemingly, information presented in a group of three remains in our head better than other sized groups; even twos. It may because three is the smallest number we need to create a pattern.

This may also be why politicians, writers and people in the marketing arena, among others, use this principle a great deal.

For example, in the UK, the Brexit campaign produced a number of political slogans like: '*Take Back Control*' and '*Get Brexit Done*'. In the USA, there have similarly been a number of three-word slogans, such as '*Yes We Can*' and '*Four More Years*'.

Marketing is littered with examples: '*Every Little Helps*', '*Finger Lickin' Good*' and '*Beanz Means, Heinz*', to name but a few. If you have worked out which companies they refer to, they have had the desired effect.

A couple of my favourites (translated from Latin into English) are: the Olympic motto – '*Swifter, Higher, Stronger*', which sums up the power, determination and ambition that the Olympiads represent; and '*I Came, I Saw, I Conquered*' – Julius Caesar's famous quotation.

My list of examples would have to include Abraham Lincoln's famous statement in his Gettysburg Address: '*A Government of the people, by the people, for the people*'.

The final word, though, goes to Winston Churchill for: '*Never before in the field of human conflict was so much owed by so many, to so few*'.

It is my experience that an audience is unlikely to take in and remember more than three messages. Some people will argue that the figure should be five or more.

Nevertheless, I have made it central to the Oratory Aide-Memoire at Part III, and I recommend that you adopt this rule, at least in your early public speaking days.

Because, if you structure your talk around threes, not least of all you will find it easier to remember and it will be more memorable to your listeners.

Summary

By the end of your analysis, you should have worked out, in outline, what you are going to say and in what order you are going to get those messages across.

You should also have concluded what clothes you will wear, what sort of atmosphere you will need to create and how best to engage your audience.

It is now time to get into the other preparations you are going to have to make.

CHAPTER 2 – PREPARATIONS

Intelligence Gathering

You will have seen in the analysis that I have encouraged you to find out all you can about the people you are going to talk to and the place where you are doing so.

No self-respecting soldiers will carry out a mission without gaining as much intelligence as they can about the target and its location. You should do the same.

When it comes to the content of your talk, there is much you can do by way of research, to help improve it.

Are there any relevant and noteworthy facts and statistics that support your messages? Are there any jokes that you might be able to use that relate, however remotely, to what you are going to say? Can you find any quotations that will support your messages and that your audience will relate to?

Being well informed is invariably in your hands and it will make your performance so much the better.

Try to find out things that the audience will not know, so that you can give them a better understanding of your subject. Or if it's something they are likely to know a little about, put your points across from your own, different, perspective.

You ought to come across as the expert on your subject matter, so you need to educate yourself accordingly.

Recce

There is an old military adage: *'time spent in reconnaissance is seldom wasted'*.

Before any serious operation, military commanders will almost certainly carry out a recce. They will get as close as they can to the target and gain as much intelligence as possible. It can sometimes mean the difference between success and failure.

It is not often that you get the chance to recce the venue you are going to speak in. But, this should not prevent you from trying to do so, if you can.

If you can't actually visit the place, then at least speak to the person arranging the engagement and get them to describe the venue. They may be able to walk around it and video stream it back to you. You may also find, if it is large enough, that there are images of it on the Internet.

At the very least, you should arrive early for your speaking engagement and make sure you go into the auditorium for at least a few minutes. During that time, you should get a feel for the place, the lectern, the technological arrangements for sound and vision and the lighting.

You should also try to speak to the person running any of those systems, so that you can build up a quick rapport and give them any instructions that you need to.

If you find that the audience is some distance away from the speaker on the stage, see if you can get closer. Distance is definitely a barrier to interaction, so try to avoid it if you can.

Just check also that your laptop, if you are using it, is compatible and has the right leads for the venue's systems. If you are bringing your slides and videos on a disk or USB stick, similarly make sure that the venue has the software to open all your media material.

Anything you can do to make your audience more comfortable, like getting the room temperature right, will help your cause.

A recce of the venue will have the added benefit of making you feel more confident. Being familiar with the place will allow you to picture yourself there as you rehearse your speech.

Training and Rehearsal

Woodrow Wilson, the US President, was once asked, '*How long does it take you to prepare a ten-minute speech?*' '*Two weeks*', he answered. *'How about a one-hour speech?' 'One week'*, he said. "*What about a two-hour speech?' 'I'm ready now!'* he replied.

There is an important lesson here. Anyone can waffle for as long as they like but, if you want to be concise, you are going to have to train yourself to be so.

Incidentally, when we are speaking publicly at an event, we say on average about 120-150 words per minute. Therefore, a 15-minute speech will be between 1,800-2,250 words – a useful statistic to have in your back pocket when you start writing your talk.

Preparation is absolutely key to your success in this arena, because you can guarantee that, before every really good speech, there has been a large amount of training and rehearsal.

There is a reason why soldiers, when they are not on operations, spend their time training in barracks or out in the field on so-called 'exercises'.

When you train, you learn lessons. When you put those lessons into practice, you improve.

Similarly, when you carry out a speaking engagement, it will invariably not go exactly as you had anticipated. Things will go wrong and you will learn from that and put them right the next time.

The problem is that your speaking engagements may be few and far between. So, you may have to generate your own exercises to give yourself practice.

Task yourself with a fictional speaking engagement that might realistically come your way. Start with something relatively easy. For example, you might prepare yourself for an interview to get into university or college, or to get a job.

After that, try a longer, more complex speech of, say, 10 minutes. Choose a subject that you know well and go through all the stages in this book, step by step.

Each time, it will give you the opportunity to go through the analysis and come up with an outline plan for what you are going to say.

Then write your speech and rehearse it (we'll cover how to do these in Part II).

Do these exercises as often as you can and vary the scenarios.

You will soon find that you start to get into a rhythm, and putting together a speech will not be as daunting as it first appears, particularly if you use the Oratory Aide-Memoire at Part III.

In summary, don't forget the real benefits of the Seven Ps. They certainly do prevent a poor performance.

The more prepared you are, the more confident you will be in your ability to deliver a successful speech.

CHAPTER 3 – SCHEME OF MANOEUVRE

Introduction

Having been through your analysis, which may have taken you a while, as all the answers to your questions are not necessarily at hand, you now need to move on to constructing your talk.

The analysis is supposed to have been your mind clearing activity. If you have not got a clear idea of the broad content and feel for your talk at this stage, you may need to do a bit more analysis.

Army commanders call the next thing they consider their 'Scheme of Manoeuvre'. It expands the intentions of the commander to describe how he or she sees the operation unfolding. It explains where, when, how and with what, in relation to each other, the force is to achieve its purpose.

It sounds a little complex, but it is actually all about clarity, so that everyone ends up on the same song sheet.

Public speakers need their own version of a scheme of manoeuvre – when are they going to say things at what part of their talk and in what manner.

In other words, what is the structure of the talk, how much is going to be said on each message, with what type of emphasis, and when are slides and videos going to be used, if at all.

It is now that you focus on all your important points and think through how you are going to make them just as important to your audience.

What you are after is to set out your theme (your 'purpose' and why you are so taken by it) and then follow up with a number of arguments, (your main messages), by way of evidence, that back up your thesis.

All the time, you are looking for the common ground between you and your listeners.

Beware the danger of including too much detail. You will find it difficult to link it all together and, more importantly, you will risk losing your audience.

I find it easiest to select some key words around which I construct the talk. These invariably turn into my main messages and are central in expressing my ideas. We'll come back to this later.

After sorting out your structure you should turn your thoughts to what you should look like and sound like on the day – your style.

I'll cover all of this in the rest of this chapter.

To keep it very simple, I recommend you break your talk down into: Beginning, Middle and End. Others use the terms: Introduction, Body and Close. It's a well tried and tested method, and it will help you get underway immediately.

I have used this approach in my Oratory Aide-Memoire at Part III.

Beginning

The beginning of your talk is the part where you captivate your audience. It's as simple as that. You need to attract them to you as a person and get them interested in what you are going to say.

It's what you say at the beginning that will make you particularly credible to your audience or not.

If you can also make your audience aware that you understand why they have come to listen to you and what they hope to get out of your talk, then that would be a bonus. You should have worked this out during your analysis.

Ice Breaker

In many ways the ice breaker, right at the beginning, is the most critical part of your talk.

It's the time when you get your audience firmly on your side, by getting them to trust you and to like you.

It's like the first paragraph of a book – if you are not grabbed by it, you're likely to put it down.

It's fundamentally your attention grabber.

So, don't make your audience wait to see how good you are. Get straight in and win them over.

A bit like a sniper, you've got one shot at this, so make it a good one.

Various researchers and psychologists have looked at this subject and most of them conclude that not only do people come to a judgement on their speaker in an extremely short time, but that, for 90% of them, their first impression does not change, even after hearing the rest of the talk.

There are a number of ways to break the ice, and you should decide which of them is most suitable for your particular audience.

Some people use a powerful image or a prop to cross this first bridge.

Others will frame a story or idea that will grab their audience's attention and at the same time tell them why they are there.

For many the first thing they use is humour. If you do, you might start with a self-deprecating joke like this well-used one: *'Before coming here tonight, I was discussing my talk with my girlfriend and she said to me, "Don't try to be too charming, too witty or too intellectual, just be yourself."* (pause for laughter) *It's times like that when I remind her she is only my current girlfriend!'*

Alternatively, you could try to engage audience with something interesting to them, as well as relevant to them. A well-tried method to do this is to ask the members of the audience to *'Raise your hand if…'*

Sometimes, using the lead-in of '*Did anyone read the article this morning in the newspaper on…?*', works well to get everyone engaged.

Whichever method you decide to use, you should practice it, so that you can use it without notes or the need to stand behind a lectern.

It's probably only going to take you less than a minute, but if you seize your audience now, you will be set fair for the rest of your talk.

Hook

Most people will stop listening to your talk within 10 minutes, unless they think there's something in it for them. So, tell them why they need to hear about this matter from you, as well as pay attention to what you are about to say – this is your hook.

Some use a shocking statistic or an appalling assertion, or ask their audience a rhetorical question on the main subject.

If you do use statistics, make sure you understand them and that are up-to-date and come from a reliable source. You may be questioned on them.

You could be bold enough to use a current catch phrase. However, it has to be convincing, as well as brief and, of course, interesting. People enjoy catch phrases and, by their nature, they are memorable.

Another popular approach is to get your audience to trigger their imagination and to create their own mental image of something, by using the words: '*Picture if you will…*' or '*Imagine for a moment…*'

Finally, you might simply use a famous and authentic quotation that will help people understand the essence of your talk.

Remember, what you're trying to do is to grab their attention, whet their appetite and persuade them that you are worth listening to.

Scene Setting

It may have been Aristotle, again, although there are other likely contenders, but there is a saying that is often repeated by public speakers concerning the art of a speech making: '*Tell them what you are going to tell them, tell them, then tell them what you told them.*'

It's generally regarded as good advice. The first part comes at this stage of your talk.

In telling them about your talk, ask yourself what's the one thing you want your audience to remember tomorrow? It's why you are speaking to them, so this should not be a difficult question.

It is here, very early on, that you need the audience to understand why you are speaking to them and why it is so important to you and to them. It's your purpose.

If your goal is not clear to you, it won't be to your audience, so spend time getting your words as specific and detailed as necessary. As you learnt in the analysis, when you write down your purpose, begin it with the word 'To…'.

You need a compelling opener that will be certain of capturing your audience's attention. It should preferably be a theme that will allow you to keep their attention throughout, as you move from one point to the next.

For example, you might say. '*This evening I'm going to talk about personal values; values that saved my life on operations and could, one day, save yours.*'

Middle

This is the heart of your talk. It's where you get across to your audience the evidence of why it is you are talking to them and why what you are saying to them should be as important to them as it is to you.

Here you make your case by setting out your ideas and getting the audience to think about things your way, now and in the future.

It's essential, therefore, that you give this section a large percentage of your attention. You will find it relatively easy to come up with an ice breaker and a hook, but it is your messages that you want them to remember and not your witty introduction.

Messages

I have chosen two revealing quotations to get this important aspect of the speech underway.

The first is by John Ford, the American film director, who said: *'You can speak well if your tongue can deliver the message of your heart.'*

And the second is by Albert Einstein, the theoretical physicist, who said that: *'If you can't explain it simply, you don't understand it well enough.'*

Speaking from your heart and in simple, deliberate terms are two winning ways of getting your messages across.

You should try not to be emotional, but you should be passionate.

I am recommending that you stick to three main messages, at least in your first few speeches. When you get more experienced, you may well wish to stretch to more. I still don't!

Whatever you do, restrict your subject matter to the time available, so you are not rushing at the end. It's always easier to end early rather than to try to cram everything in.

You should plan on taking your audience on a journey through your messages, using them to explain what you want them to know.

Each message must have a direct relationship to your main theme, be that a premise, a theory or an argument.

They should also be clearly linked to each other and be in a logical sequence.

The messages should resonate with your audience and appeal to the heart as well as the mind.

Your choice of words is important to getting your messages across in the manner in which you want them understood. So, spend time 'wordsmithing' your text until you hone it satisfactorily.

Deliver ideas that are understandable and believable. This way your audience will 'own' them and you will have no difficulty in persuading them.

Keep your messages brief, specific and, if possible, actionable. These are the points of your talk that you particularly want them to remember and, if you're lucky, repeat elsewhere.

Your messages may need reinforcing with other information. This will not always be the case but, again, I recommend that you have no more than three supporting points per main message.

You should make your points, illustrate them with examples, experience and stories and then restate your point on closing.

Anything that has an element of human interest goes down well; so personal anecdotes are more convincing than other approaches.

We will come to how you put your messages across, (as well as the rest of your talk) in Part II.

Until then, remember what Lord Reading once said about speechmaking: *'Always be shorter than anybody dared to hope.'*

End

It's important that you give the ending of your talk due consideration. Let's face it, just like the ending in movies, plays, songs and books, it is critical.

Some people advise that you simply end by thanking your audience for listening. But, for me, the ending is an integral and key part of your speech and what you hope to achieve in giving it.

It will not surprise you that, once more, I am recommending that you stick to the rule of three to finish powerfully and memorably.

Quick Summary

This is the time when you 'tell them what you've told them.' It needs to be quick and concise. It's the sort of thing you would say if you were asked what your speech was all about.

Remind people why you and they came today and what your thesis is, and highlight what the benefits will be to those in the audience, elsewhere or in the world as a whole.

Some Humour

Try to keep something especially funny for the end, so that you finish on a high. A great joke or an engaging and amusing tale makes the audience feel warm at just the right time.

It's worth having a short and a long tale up your sleeve so that you can use one or other depending on the time available.

If you are no good at humour, then use a suitably famous quotation that really sums up your subject matter.

Call to Action

It's not too dramatic to say that you should end with some stirring words that your audience will remember, just like they would remember the ending of a good film.

When you get more experienced, you will find that you jump to this part of your speech very early on in the planning. In a nutshell, it's why you are you speaking.

It will be the culmination of all the stories you have related throughout your speech and will, in effect, be what you set out to do in the beginning.

Try to describe the impact of what would change if your listeners took on board what you have said.

Your aim is to make sure your audience leaves thinking 'I'm going to do something about that'.

You need to deliver your call to action in a powerful, memorable and inspirational way; speaking with emphasis and passion and driving home your request.

Style

In your scheme of manoeuvre, you will have put in place almost all the bits of the jigsaw puzzle that is your speech. However, it is essential that you don't leave out a very important piece – your style.

How you look and how you sound can influence greatly what your audience thinks about you as a person and as a speaker.

Ultimately, these things may have a big effect on how well your speech, and what you say in it, is accepted.

Tone

A famous Armenian born professor, Albert Mehrabian, believes that there are three core elements of effective face-to-face communication.

He came up with the so-called 7%-38%-55% communication rule. It states that 7% of meaning is communicated through the spoken word, 38% through the tone of the voice and 55% through body language.

Tone enables you to speak with conviction and to convince people about what you are saying.

It needs, therefore, to be a fundamental characteristic of any public speaker.

Tone is how we describe the emotional quality of speaking, and there are only three alternatives: positive, negative or neutral.

Your words and actions contribute to the overall energy and happiness in your listeners. If you are negative, pessimistic and sarcastic, it will turn them off.

Obviously, a public speaker needs always to adopt the positive tone. It is one that is clearer, because it uses fewer words and its phrasing is simpler.

Using a positive tone will help get people to buy into your ideas and it will establish a good rapport with them.

All you need to do at this stage of your preparations is to think through how you are going to adopt a thoroughly positive tone, based on what you have learned about your audience and the venue.

Posture/Bearing

Bearing is a fairly old-fashioned word, although one that is still regular used in the British Army. It's simply describes a person's way of standing or moving.

Interestingly, if you look up the word posture, the dictionary talks about the *'position in which someone holds their body when standing or sitting'*.

There are a few things you should avoid when speaking in front of an audience: stooped shoulders; head bowed down; hands in pockets; swaying body; shifting feet; and leaning on objects, like the lectern.

It stands to reason, therefore, that you should strive to: stand up straight; look the audience in the eye; and keep your arms and hands ready to help you highlight a point. By doing these things you will remove any distractions that your posture or bearing might lead to.

I have never done it, but years ago they used to teach people to rehearse their speeches with books on their head. I think it's probably worth having a try, just to see what happens to your posture.

Appearance

Apparently, we stereotype people within 10 seconds of meeting them. We quickly decide fundamental things about them and their lifestyle.

Like it or not, people judge each other on what they are wearing. So, being appropriately dressed is critical if you wish to respect and not to alienate your audience.

Anyway, people will be put off what you are saying if your clothes are too distracting.

Some say you should raise your game by one level. So, if you normally wear a T-shirt, then put on a shirt with a collar for a change, and wear shoes, not trainers.

Whatever you do, you should at least dress to match the level at which your audience has dressed, otherwise you will lose credibility.

Another piece of advice you get is to wear contrasting colours if you wish to sound more authoritative and powerful. I can't vouch for this.

Like your body language, posture is all about your non-verbal communication. It is an important element of the whole and it needs to be treated as such.

Summary of Part I

Planning and preparation are absolute musts for soldiers and they are equally important for people about to engage in public speaking.

By the time you get to this stage in the proceedings, you will have done a great deal to get the bedrock of your speech set fair.

If you skip any part of the scientific process of analysis, you risk failing on the day. Just remember what the acronym 'Seven Ps' stands for.

Don't underestimate the time these preparations will take you, if done properly, particularly for your first few speeches. Fear not, things will speed up as you get more proficient.

By the time you have done these preparations you should be very clear on a number of things: the venue, your audience and what you are going to say.

You will also have a plan of action – your beginning, middle and end.

In particular, you will have nailed down your messages – why they are so important and where they will fit into your speech as a whole.

You are now ready to tackle the important part of exactly 'how' you are going to put your plan into action; or what soldiers call the 'execution'.

PART II

EXECUTION

CHAPTER 4 – TACTICS

The parallels between military operations and public speaking begin to widen at this stage. However, in both activities, it is important to get 'how' you are going to deliver your plan just right.

Soldiers make use of tactics to carry out their operations. They are based upon years of practical experience and have developed to meet changes in weaponry, technology and communications, among other things.

Similarly, experienced public speakers have created the equivalent of tactics for their profession.

First Impressions

The initial tactic you should employ is to ensure that you create a really good first impression with your audience.

All audiences will size you up, and individuals will come to a quick conclusion about you. Some will do this even before you speak, but most will wait.

They will decide: whether you are confident in what you are saying and the way in which you are saying it; whether you are a passionate about your subject matter; whether they can trust you and your messages; and whether you are a likeable person – one that is intelligent, warm and a kind human being.

First impressions last, so make them good ones, such that your audience is hanging on your every word thereafter.

You need to think this through during your analysis. Ask yourself what sort of impression you want to make on them. Then ask yourself 'so what?'. This will lead you to 'how' you are going to do it.

Also ask yourself what sort of a mood you want to create in the room…and 'so what?'.

You do this analysis because it then gives you the power to control the first impression on which your audience will judge you.

We talked about your style earlier, and that will go some way towards creating the right impression; quite a long way, in fact.

Your facial expression will also play a part, so come on with a natural and confident smile, making eye contact with the audience and keeping it up thereafter.

If you have any doubts, get someone to video you rehearsing your speech and watch it back with the sound off. You'll instantly realise that it's your face everyone concentrates on.

You want your talk to be lively and informative. It should also arouse their curiosity, particularly at the beginning.

You should minimise the use of 'um', 'ah', 'like' and 'you know'. They can distract the audience and give the impression that you are unsure of yourself.

First impressions are so important that, like the break-in battle on military operations, they need your special attention.

Working with Your Audience

The next phase of your plan will be to deliver your messages strongly and convincingly. To do that, you will need to keep your audience with you as you journey through your stories.

There is a very apt quotation from Maya Angelou, an American poet, memoirist, and civil rights activist. *'I've learned that people will forget what you said, people will forget what you did, but people will never forget how you made them feel.'*

Once you have captured your audience, therefore, your next tactic is akin to guarding your prisoners. Do not to let them escape. Working on their emotions is the most likely way in which you will be successful.

To do so, you will need to be aware of your audience and why they are listening to you.

You should strive to build a rapport with them and develop a chemistry between you.

Just think of those speakers who have engaged with you and motivated you; they will have had warmth and sincerity, plenty of confidence and charisma, and they will have projected an impressive image. You need to be and do the same.

Get them to identify with you; and get them involved in your talk, intellectually.

Do, however, make it as natural as possible.

Just beware, when you try to engage with your audience, the people in it may not be as you expected and you may have to alter your approach accordingly.

Your job is to interact with your listeners so that you make them see the vision you have and, hopefully, do something about it.

This is best summed up in a quotation, the origins of which I cannot recall: '*You measure the impact of your words, not only on the beauty or emotion of the moment but on whether you change the way people not only think but the way they feel.*'

Converse with your audience. To do that you need to make them feel you are having a conversation with them and that they are being consulted. Question them, challenge them and even 'argue' with them. Grab their attention, monitor their reactions and react to them.

When you are speaking, maintain eye contact with your audience. If the room is large, keep your eyes moving from the front to the back and from left to the right. It helps some people to think of the auditorium as a large capital letter M, and their eyes move from point to point.

If you are in a very large auditorium you should move your head like a slowly sweeping spotlight, left to right and back again. That way you will cover your entire audience.

Storytelling

Clearly, there are a number of ways soldiers can execute their operations. Similarly, there are different ways in which speakers can get their messages across to their audiences.

By far the most highly regarded is the art of storytelling.

Long before humans could read and write they were telling stories to communicate.

At its base, storytelling is simply a process of communicating a narrative to your audience. It often includes facts, but you can make a story more elaborate by embellishing it, to explain your message more effectively.

There's an old saying penned by the author and coach Ed Percival, I believe: '*Never tell a story without making a point and never make a point without telling a story.*'

Use your stories to drive home the messages.

The reason people use storytelling is because stories are more memorable and more personal. They can, therefore, be more persuasive.

The best stories get people's interest. They engage them so that they continue to listen. They also teach them something and they motivate them to do something positive.

So, when you are telling a story to explain one of your main messages, keep those objectives in the back of your mind.

As you tell a story, you will be connecting on an emotional level, particularly if you relate how you feel about your message. If it's something from your own life experiences, that's even better, especially if you can get the listeners to feel the way you feel.

Tell a story that you are interested in and build it up so that the ending is something you and your audience can sympathise with.

The exceptional stories are ones that your audience will easily understand and relate to. They are the ones the listeners will recall and retell tomorrow.

Incidentally, we are particularly moved by stories about one person, an individual. Bear this in mind when you are developing the stories concerning your messages.

Stories, like speeches, have a beginning, middle and end, and often have winners and losers.

In the beginning you spell out what's at stake and what the risks are, in the middle you discuss the problems and struggles (and the tension rises) then at the end there is some sort of solution.

It's unlikely that you can build suspense and end with a cliff hanger, but keep the intrigue going as your message develops, if at all possible.

Whenever you can, put in the unexpected, such that the audience thinks 'I didn't know that'.

You should, of course, usually use stories to help your listeners visualise what you are saying. Alternatively, frame your stories into questions and you will, naturally, create a conversation.

Picking which story best fits which of your messages is the tricky task, because your story has also to be their story.

Script or No Script?

Soldiers sometimes have to make a choice between a silent attack, using stealth and surprise, or a noisy attack, using air, artillery and other support from the start.

It's not a direct correlation, but it is almost as important as the decision that you will have to make concerning whether or not you use a script during your speech. Success may depend on it.

There are basically three ways of delivering a speech: learn it by heart and recite it from memory; use notes for reference; and read it directly from a script.

The pros and cons of using a script or not are obvious, but they are worth listing.

If you don't read from a script: you look more confident and authentic; your credibility rises; you seem more natural and spontaneous; your direct contact forces the audience to pay more attention to what you are saying; you're not tied to a lectern, so you are free to use the stage (and the auditorium) to be entirely informal and reactive; eye-to-eye contact allows you to put your messages across with passion; you are able to interact better with your audience; you are able to sound more informal and conversational; you are able to read your audience's reaction as you progress; it makes it easier for you to adjust what you're saying if your audience's reaction is not going the way you expected; you are able to think on your feet, which your audience will notice and appreciate. Although, it's harder work preparing for and rehearsing a speech without a script.

That said, if you do read from a script: you are less likely to forget where you are in your speech or go 'off piste', which can lead to embarrassing pauses and missed messages; you have less chance of going blank or losing your train of thought altogether; and you will probably be standing behind a lectern and so getting some reassurance that that brings.

Clearly, the disadvantages of reading from a script far outweigh the advantages of doing so. I suppose that was obvious.

If you need further persuading, just remember what your mother and father did to put you to sleep when you were a child.

Despite all that, if you are new to public speaking, it is a particularly brave decision not to use a script, so I am going to suggest ways to help you avoid doing so.

There is an obvious halfway house – the use of notes. This is a good first step towards the completely unaided performance.

It's a bit like carrying out a silent attack, but having artillery standing by ready to give you support.

My Oratory Aide-Memoire at Part III is designed to help you do just that.

I would recommend its use by all bar the extremely confident speakers or the intensely nervous.

Contingency Planning

It is incumbent on all military commanders, when planning operations, to ask themselves a number of 'what ifs?' What if phase 1 of a 3-phase operation is not successful? What if the enemy appears in strength from a position that we didn't consider or are too strong to overcome?

These will be questions, which will mainly consider eventualities that would cause the operation as a whole to fail, that will warrant some form of contingency plan.

Similarly, public speakers need to have thought through and decided how they would deal with situations that have major effects on their speeches.

In practice, there are two main things that would badly knock a speaker off his or her stride: a persistent interruption from one or more people in the audience; or losing the thread of the talk to the extent that they dry up.

There are also some less serious things that will cause the speaker to lose his or her flow: the microphone stops working; the slides do not appear when expected; the lights go out; the audience does not react in the way the speaker expected; members of the audience start walking out; the talk runs badly over its time allowance. There will undoubtedly be others.

The most important thing you need to do is to 'think on your feet'. Soldiers have to do this all the time, because they work on the basis that nothing will go to plan after the first bullet is fired.

Rudyard Kipling in his famous poem '*If*' talked about it: '*If you can keep your head when all about you are losing theirs and blaming it on you...*'

Thinking on your feet is a matter of keeping a clear head. Don't allow yourself to be overwhelmed by your situation. Breathe in deeply and think things through logically. Don't panic!

If you have dried up, picture in your mind the progression you made when you put the speech together. This should bring back the messages.

Managing the more minor activities should be relatively simple, although they all need to be considered.

If the microphone fails, ask that the organisers try to fix it, meanwhile try to continue by speaking louder.

If the slides stop appearing, pause and give the organisers a chance to fix the issue, but be prepared to press on by describing your slides at the times they would appear.

Unless you are reading from a script, losing the lights should not be too disturbing. The organisers should be able to produce a torch or other form of light to help you read your notes.

In short, you should do all you can to press on with your talk while others try to sort out the issues.

It is the same with a minor interruption from your audience. A solitary outburst should not prevent you carrying on. Just ignore it.

On balance, I would recommend that you do not engage in any form of conversation with those intent on interrupting your talk. Your best approach is to remain silent while the organisers and, perhaps, the remainder of your audience deal with the interrupters.

Stand-up comedians tend to take on interrupters, using more humour to attack them. You will not necessarily have that sort of ammunition in your pouch, so you are almost certainly going to better off keeping your head down.

If you find yourself being hurried up by the organisers or, more likely, for whatever reason you have much less time than you thought for your speech, don't panic.

You should do a swift analysis of the situation and a quick time calculation to determine how you are going to fit in what you need to say.

Depending on when you find out about the shortening of your time, you must obviously get your messages across and probably your call to action. They are the central parts of what you are saying. The sub points may have to be left out or paraphrased.

CHAPTER 5 – SKILLS

Confidence

There is a very old saying that '*The average person at a funeral would rather be in the casket than giving the eulogy*'.

I'm sure this is true but, don't worry, as author Mark Twain used to say: '*There are two types of speakers: those who get nervous and those who are liars.*'

Being nervous is natural and normal. You may well feel this: '*The human brain starts working the moment you are born and never stops until you stand up to speak in public.*' George Jessel, the American actor, singer, songwriter, film producer and comedic entertainer.

It's normal to feel self-conscious and to suffer so-called 'stage fright'. Some 90% of us initially suffer from both of these.

There are several reasons why we might feel nervous. We fear: that we are going to forget our words and train of thoughts; that we are not good enough at public speaking to come across well; that our audience is not going to like what we have to say; that people are going to hate the way we are dressed and how we look in general; and that people will not like our voices.

All these are logical concerns, but none of them is impossible to fix. It's just because we are up in front of an audience that we suddenly become more conscious of them.

Voice coaches, among others, will tell you that all speaking is public speaking, whether it's to one person or many hundreds. Somehow, we have to believe that concept and thus gain the confidence we need to talk to an audience.

All of us have the confidence in us. That's where it exists – within. We just need to find it and develop the skill to invoke it when required.

Basically, it's our fear and we can control it.

Know Your Plan

'*Only the prepared speaker deserves to be confident.*' Dale Carnegie, the American writer and lecturer.

It's important not to get overwhelmed by the task ahead. The military have processes and procedures so that, when the pressure is on, they can still be decisive.

The plan that you put together in your analysis and the detail that you put on it in your scheme of manoeuvre will certainly stand you in good stead. It will give you the confidence to know that you are well prepared.

When you get to the time when you take that plan and rehearse it, that's when you really become self-confident about the upcoming talk.

If you want to speak confidently you must know your subject matter inside out; so, rehearse, rehearse, rehearse.

Put simply, the better you know your subject matter and the order in which you are going to say things, the more confident your performance will be.

Combatting Fear

Statistically, it isn't that often that people badly mess up a speech. Yet, we all think that we are going to do so. Indeed, we sometimes picture everything going wrong and it all ending in tears.

A fear of public speaking is not rare. Even seasoned speakers can get a bout of nerves.

But, we can cope with our fear of public oratory and feel more at ease with being the centre of attention in a few, well-regarded, ways.

A number of factors lead to nervousness, not least of all the hormones that your body releases when you start to get stressed.

You will particularly notice it when adrenaline starts coursing through your body. It makes your heart rate increase, it can cause you to perspire and makes your breathing become fast and shallow.

Not surprisingly, you will then most likely talk quickly, which will increase your chances of stumbling over your words.

However, if you use the adrenaline flow and redirect this self-inflicted pressure to your advantage, it can be very positive. So, don't fight your nerves.

Firstly, before you go on stage, start to take deep breaths. When you are out there, continue to take deep breaths as a matter of course. This will slow your heart rate and counter the stress your situation places on you.

It will have the knock-on effect of causing you to speak more slowly and to pause on occasion. Pauses make you sound more natural, confident and authentic.

Some people recommend that you should carry out a number of physical exercises before you go on stage. I have never done this, so I cannot comment. However, if lying on the floor doing relaxation exercises works for you, then go ahead.

If you feel a little wobbly, as you come on stage, make yourself feel more secure by holding onto the lectern or standing next to something solid. Don't do this for long; just enough to bolster yourself.

Secondly, try to think positively. It is because you are concentrating on yourself and how nervous you feel that you get yourself into a vicious circle.

You really need to focus on practically anything other than yourself. The more you concentrate on other things, the more confident you will feel.

Think about the audience and how, through what you have to say, you will make a positive difference to the people out there. After all, it's their needs that should matter, not yours.

Just remember, the vast majority in your audience will want your talk to go well and will inwardly be urging you on.

Whatever you do, don't apologise for your nervousness. They probably had not noticed.

Finally, if you can, concentrate on trying to converse as if you are talking to just one person in the audience. Pick out someone who looks friendly and talk to them as though they are the only one out there. Don't forget to switch from one person to another, lest the others begin to feel as if they don't matter.

Speaking

There are a number of skills you can develop to improve yourself and your performance when you are speaking in public. I have selected four common areas that I believe are worth addressing as you progress with your development.

Voice

The effective use of the voice is one of the essential skills needed by any public speaker. If your voice is monotone, listeners will think you are boring and lose interest quickly. So, do learn to modulate your voice.

We discussed earlier how important tone is to your speech making, given the Mehrabian rule of communication. Additionally, there are ways to use one's voice to best effect.

Your voice has got to be interesting, so vary the pitch, use different tones and pause for effect.

Pauses can be particularly effective at increasing the impact of what you have just said. They can also cause your audience to anticipate what you are going to say next. They, therefore, have an important part to play in your public speaking.

You definitely need to be a 'cup half full person' to be a successful public speaker, so your voice needs to reflect that positivity and be upbeat.

That said, you need to be yourself, otherwise the listeners will see through you and you'll lose their trust.

You should try to create a warm and positive connection with your audience, keeping your voice strong and clear throughout.

If you are going to be credible, deliver your messages with conviction. This way you will earn the audience's respect very early on.

Projecting your voice is at the end of a long mental and vocal process and it starts with getting your thoughts in order. So, practice doing just that.

Overly verbose speakers can be both boring and frustrating to listen to, so be concise.

Changing the volume of your voice is an effective way to emphasise certain points. Whereas, speaking too slowly can be tedious, and the audience may stop paying attention.

Speak loud enough and clearly enough for your audience to hear, without shouting.

Modulate your voice so that you are not speaking in a monotone, which will make you sound like a dull and uninteresting person.

Use your voice to change the emotions of your audience. This way you will not only change the way the people in your audience think but also the way they feel.

Finally, your voice needs to relaxed, engaging and expressive.

There seems to be a lot to think about concerning your voice, but a little practice will work wonders.

Timing

We have discussed how nervousness will make you speed up and rush through what you are saying, as the adrenalin courses through your body.

There is a misconception that we always need to fill every moment with sound.

The general rule is to try to speak more slowly than you think is necessary. Use your breathing to regulate your speed and put in more pauses than you would otherwise. In this way, you should dictate the pace of your talk.

If you also pause for effect, you will allow the audience to grasp what you have said; it's a powerful piece of timing.

Finally, make use of rhythm to lead your audience to the important points you are making, all the time building to a highpoint.

Body Language

Speakers need to send out the right signals to their audience. The signals need to be open, encouraging the audience to trust you.

Your body language is your way of communicating with your audience without speaking.

When we look at a speaker, we see whether he or she is relaxed, calm and confident and is obviously at ease with their subject.

It's really all about self-assurance. You need to hide your nerves and exude an air of authority. Because, if you are comfortable in your own skin, you will make your audience comfortable too.

Your posture will help, so don't slouch at the lectern and don't fidget with anything on it or in your pockets.

You need to come across as being relaxed and confident, even if you are not.

We know that eye contact helps a speaker's credibility and their ability to convey interest and warmth. Pausing for a couple of seconds on an individual before moving on to another is a good rule of thumb.

Combine that with the right sort of facial expression and people will want to listen.

Your face, more than any other part of you, will communicate to those listening to you how you are feeling in yourself and about what you're saying.

Apparently, there are no less than 21 facial expressions.

The most obvious expression is that of smiling or a happy expression. Having come on to the stage smiling you should try to smile frequently throughout your speech. It will make you more attractive in the broadest sense.

A smiling person has warmth and approachability. Others are more comfortable around that sort of person and will listen to them more intently.

Finally, nerves can cause your voice and your face to tense up, which will impede your speech and the manner in which you project it. Relax!

Movement

Move about as much as you can. Don't get pinned down behind a lectern. One way to do this is to leave your notes in one place and move to another.

It's almost impossible to speak passionately and yet not move around.

You will also want to use your hands to express your passion. Use both hands to illustrate points, but don't overuse the gestures. They need to be used for effect and not just to give them something to do, otherwise they will become distracting.

It's all about engaging your audience rather than turning them off because you are lifeless.

Working with Words

The word 'eloquence' is not used as much as it once was, but great speakers are eloquent. It's the ability to speak fluently and persuasively. It's all about the skill of finding the right words and language that will convince the audience.

Words have the power to stir people. They help you paint pictures and draw on the imagination.

The liberal use of certain figures of speech can do just that and you should develop your skills in using them.

There may be 250 or more figures of speech, but you can probably limit your use of them to two or three of the better-known ones, to help bring memorable images to your audience.

Metaphors and Similes

A metaphor is a figure of speech that is used to make a comparison between two things that aren't alike but do have something in common. In effect they create a bridge or connection between the new and the familiar and should help you give a new perspective on things.

Famous metaphors include: *the world is a stage; you are my sunshine; laughter is the music of the soul;* and *it's raining cats and dogs.*

They are very good at painting pictures in your audiences' minds. It is one of the easiest ways for you to conjure up an image about what you are saying. They also make you, the speaker, far more engaging.

Obviously, the metaphors you use need to be relevant and targeted at your audience. If, for example, they are a group of young people, don't use a metaphor that's dated or old-fashioned. That's similar to dad-dancing!

It is often best just to use one particular metaphor a number of times throughout your talk. This will ensure that your audience better understands it and remembers what you have said.

A simile is a figure of speech that is an interesting way of comparing one thing with another thing of a different kind.

The words 'like' or 'as' are usually involved in the simile, which is not the case in metaphors.

Well-used examples of similes are: *as clear as mud; as brave as a lion; and as clean as a whistle.*

So, a simile makes a direct comparison: *she is as innocent as an angel*, whereas a metaphor's comparison is implied but not stated: *she is an angel.*

That has been a bit of a vocabulary lesson, but it is well worth your while making sure you understand it. Using figures of speech is a very well tried and tested method of getting one's views across effectively.

Repetition

We don't usually like to use repetition when we are speaking. It's not natural. However, it is an excellent and powerful tool if you use it in the right context. The skill in using it is certainly worth developing in your public speaking.

In its simplest form, there are many everyday phrases we use that are repetitive: *time after time; heart to heart; hour to hour; over and over.*

Repetition is simply the reuse of words, ideas, phrases, themes or messages. It helps you bring attention to and highlight your points, such that the audience is far more likely to remember them.

Repeating a message, for example, will allow you to emphasise it and should get your audience to understand how important it is.

Plan on also using this tactic when your audience is not paying attention. It will help them stay alert.

There are innumerable examples of the use of repetition, from which I have selected just two.

Martin Luther King famously repeated the phrase '*I have a dream*' in his speech in Alabama in 1963.

Winston Churchill regularly used repetition in his speeches in Parliament. On one occasion he said: '*...we shall defend our Island, whatever the cost may be, we shall fight on the beaches, we shall* *fight on the landing grounds, we shall fight in the fields and in the streets, we shall fight in the hills; we shall never surrender…'*

Both these speeches are worth listening to, if only to hear how powerful the use of repetition can be.

Examples

You will be keen for your audience to grasp what your messages are as quickly and as profoundly as possible. The use of examples is a very good way of doing this, because it allows you to 'show' them something as opposed to just tell them.

Examples will help you make what might be an abstract idea more substantive, by identifying a specific case or situation.

Use personal experiences as much as possible. They bring your material to life. They also make your audience empathise with what you are saying and identify with you.

No matter how dry your subject matter, you can always find an example to humanise it.

When you use examples, keep them short and concise, so that you don't lose the audience's attention. Unlike humorous tales, your audience won't be hanging on for the ending.

Humour

There is a famous quotation from a poem written in 1883 by Ella Wheeler, the American author and poet, which is a valuable lesson for all public speakers: *'laugh and the world laughs with you; weep and you weep alone.'*

Getting you message across in an appealing, entertaining and informative way will doubtless get your audience on your side.

Good speakers should be able to change the emotions of their audience. They use humour to make their audience feel happy.

Getting the balance between humour and sincerity right, in the way that your audience will best receive your speech, should be your aim.

Engaging your listeners with a ready smile is the best way to start. However, a good joke can make them laugh, which is particularly winning because it makes them feel comfortable and warm.

Jokes can create a common ground and lessen the perceived difference between people.

But, only tell jokes if you are good at telling jokes. If you are not, it's best to leave them out. The silence can be deafening if your joke falls flat.

Gentle humour often works as well, if not better, in certain circumstances.

If you do decide on using a joke, the best ones are probably those that are self-deprecating or so-called ego-busters. They make a positive impression and show that you don't take yourself too seriously.

US President Ronald Reagan once remarked: '*I know you fellows think I'm lazy, but this week I've really been burning the midday oil*'.

Funny tales also work well, particularly towards the end of your talk, and may suit your audience.

On television, you'll often see stand-up comedians taking it out on one or more people in the front row. The ones that are successful are those that don't make you uncomfortable by what they are saying. Psychologically, teasing is acceptable, but bullying is not.

Unless your purpose is to entertain your audience, I recommend that you limit your jokes to one at the beginning and one at the end.

Incidentally, it has been proven that people prefer more information and less humour in the morning until about 10am; something to remember when you are doing your analysis.

Technology

The only reason you should use technology is to help you get your messages across better than you could do without it. Everything you use should add value and meaning to your talk.

It should always be regarded as a secondary factor or a backup in communicating to your audience. In other words, it should be something that follows you rather than you following it.

If you use technology, you or an assistant will need to manage it before and during your speaking engagement, so factor this in during your analysis.

Beware, if you rely on technology too much and it goes wrong, you're in trouble. Computers and projectors can crash, so always have a backup plan or a contingency, which you should have considered during your analysis.

You can research a multitude of dos and don'ts about the use of slides, music, videos and props etc. Here I am simply listing a few recommendations that most trainers of presenters would give you.

Slides and Video

You will have heard the old English adage: '*a picture is worth a thousand words*.' For a public speaker who is often trying to create a picture in the listener's mind, this is particularly important.

When you are trying to convey the meaning of something in the most effective way, you may well find yourself turning to slides or a prop and even video to back up your talk.

Visuals can certainly be a way to emotionally connect with your audience. They can undoubtedly help them remember your points.

But, do speak to your audience and not to your slides. Whatever you do, don't read them out word for word. They are there to support you and not the other way around.

Turning your back or even turning sideways on your audience is not only unattractive, but it gives your listeners the chance to look away and stop listening to you.

The much-backed rule on slides is: use graphics not text. You can say what you would write in the text and use graphics to paint the picture a little better.

Another good idea is: don't bombard your audience with statistics and graphs. Use them sparingly to best effect.

Finally, do make sure that the screen saver is turned off on your computer and that it doesn't go into sleep mode; turn off messages as well.

Props

The word prop covers everything from lecterns, flipcharts, projectors and your other audio/visual aids.

There are, of course, physical visual aids that we call props; many speakers use them.

Bill Gates, co-founder of Microsoft, once brought on stage and opened a jar out of which flew a number of mosquitos. His talk was called: *'Mosquitoes, Malaria and Education.'* I think we can assume that his audience was quite attentive thereafter.

Quite often, particularly if you are speaking in a dining room after a meal, the use of a laptop or slide projector is impracticable. You may consider using a suitably portable prop to enhance your talk.

Props can be used to: engage with the audience during the beginning of your talk, perhaps as an ice breaker; create interest and add variety; help focus the audience's attention; make your speech more memorable. They can even be substitutes for your speaking notes.

Clearly, whatever prop you use, it needs to have a direct connection with your speech, either with the theme as a whole or with one or other of your main messages. It's probably unnecessary extra work to bring on a prop just for a laugh, unless you are there to entertain the audience.

Keep your props hidden until you need them and make sure your entire audience can see them.

If you are able to surprise them with your prop, so much the better. It will make your talk all the more memorable.

Microphone

I would recommend that you only use a microphone if you have to. It's just another thing that can go wrong, and they certainly alter the sound of your voice.

However, the organisers of your talk will ask you to use one if they believe their auditorium needs it. They will know if certain areas of your audience will find it difficult to hear an unassisted speaker's voice.

If you have to use one, do so on the lowest volume possible. At least, then, you have a chance of sounding more conversational.

What you must try to avoid is shouting. It will make you sound aggressive.

Getting it the right distance away from your lips is the key.

It's a very old gag and is often used as an ice breaker, but if you test your microphone at the start of your talk by asking: '*Can you hear me at the back?*'. You can then follow it up with: '*The last time I asked that some comedian at the back shouted, Yes, I can hear you, but I would willingly swap with someone who can't.*'

CHAPTER 6 – FINAL PREPARATIONS

Let's take stock.

So far, you have carried out a comprehensive analysis of the speaking task in front of you. That analysis, combined with wider research and a recce (real or virtual) will have enabled you to come up with your outline plan.

Next, you have taken that plan and put it into a scheme of manoeuvre, giving your talk a structure and laying out what your messages and supporting points will be, as well as if and when you will use slides, videos or other aids.

You have also decided exactly how you are going to put your speech across, including what your tactics will be to get the audience behind you right from the start and to keep them onside throughout.

This will include your various storylines – the central part of your talk – as well as the general tenor of your speech.

You will also have thought through your assorted contingencies if things don't go according to plan.

We have come now to the point at which you are ready to seriously address your script.

Rehearsals

Whereas I continue to recommend that you do not read from a script, I believe that you should write your speech out in full, as a starting point.

Get it all down on paper, with everything in the right order, so that you will at least have a good idea of the extent of your talk and, having read it through, got a feel for its length.

If it's too long, cut things out at this early stage, otherwise your talk will still be too long when you have gone through the next stages.

The next step is to convert that wordy script into an outline, by going through it and highlighting the sentences or phrases that will summarise the messages and points you are making.

As you do this, make sure you fully understand the reduced wording and what has been cut out. This will start the process of embedding it in your memory.

If you prefer images, this is the time when you might think about putting your outline down in storyboard form. You should end up with something similar to the page of a comic.

It's folly to think that you can memorise the full script word for word, so do not try; unless it's a three-minute speech. If you did, you would sound wooden and unnatural. There would be a real risk that you would forget something, and the whole speech would be in danger of collapsing.

You should, however, fully learn your speech's first and last minutes – the ice breaker and the call to action. They are not parts of your speech that you should be consulting notes over.

The final stage in preparing your speech is to go through the outline and double highlight the key (and memorable) words. This will allow you to end up with useful speaking notes.

I will help you do all of this when we get to Part III, where you will learn how to put your aide-memoire together.

Armed with the highlighted outline of your talk, you are now ready to start rehearsing.

'*Practice makes perfect*', or so the saying goes. It certainly dramatically improves a public speaker.

Surprising as it may seem, even soldiers carry out rehearsals. Indeed, they are a formal part of the procedures for carrying out any operation.

Their aim is to practice the actions that are expected, so that the troops become familiar with them and get a visual impression of the tactical plan.

There are no shortcuts to rehearsing what you are going to say in a speech. Start earlier than you might think necessary, so that you don't put added pressure on yourself. This is not a *lastminute.com* activity.

You don't want to start too early, but three or four days before the event should be enough. You should plan on a number of rehearsals – at least two a day – so that you refine your talk successively until it is how you want it.

You won't be looking to make wholesale changes each time, but it will need tweaking.

Early in your rehearsals you will need to come up with strong and easily remembered links or transitions between your main messages and sub points. This will ensure that the speech flows without undue gaps.

Read through your outline a number of times so that you start to get a feel for the plan and the key messages in it.

After a while, you will start to remember the progression of the speech. When you get to that point, you can put aside the outline (don't bin it, as you may need to go back to it) and turn to your final speaking notes – your aide-memoire.

In your later rehearsals, try to make things as realistic as you can by replicating the sorts of noises and disturbances you may be subject to. At the very least, have a radio on in the background, so that you can practice thinking and talking through distractions.

If you get the chance, do a dummy run in front of a small live audience, perhaps family members. There's nothing better than a friendly crowd to give you the feedback you need to improve.

What you need to find out is if your speech is clear, interesting and convincing.

If a live audience is not possible, some suggest you seek out a full-length mirror and rehearse in front of that. I find that I am completely distracted in front of a mirror, so it is horses for courses.

Whenever possible, record your presentations and speeches on video. This will help you improve in almost every aspect: your words; the clarity and speed of your voice; your tone; your verbal stalls, such as 'um' and 'like'; your facial expressions and eye contact; your mannerisms; and your body language.

Your last rehearsal should be a dress rehearsal. Go through it in full, as you would in the real venue. Time yourself, and use all the visual aids you plan on using.

By the end of rehearsals, you need to sound conversational, so that when people hear you they feel that you are talking to them, personally.

Last Minute Preparations

'When I was getting dressed before coming out to this event this evening, I said to myself. "The last thing you must do before you leave the house is to forget your speech". And, sure enough, the last thing I did before I left the house was to forget my speech. So, it's all ad lib, I'm afraid.' Rowan Atkinson, the British actor, comedian and writer.

There are things you need to do before you leave your house or office on the way to give your speech. The first of which is to remember your speech notes, your slides and any props.

You should also make sure you are in the right clothing and that things are done up properly. Most importantly, ensure that you are confident in what you have chosen to dress in.

Do a time estimation and check the route online, if you can, to see if there are any potential holdups. Aim to arrive well before your start time, as there are a few things to do when you get to the venue.

You should understand that it is more than important, bordering on the critical, for you to be on time for your engagement. No matter what the reason for your lateness, an audience is usually unforgiving. You will be blamed for your lateness, whatever, so get there early.

If you are going to be late, make sure you contact the venue and tell them the reason, as well as the latest time of arrival. It's better to aim off than have to give a revised time later. Audiences will still not be pleased, but they will probably allow you a chance to make a good first impression.

When you get to the venue, turn your phone off; not on mute or vibrate, but off. This will bring you some peace of mind to turn your attention fully to your speaking engagement.

You should have time to go into the auditorium, talk to any assistant and run through your slides and videos. Test the microphone and the sound levels and generally get comfortable with the surroundings in which you are going to speak.

Take the chance to drink some water and to warm up your voice, perhaps by rehearsing your ice breaker.

You don't want to over-rehearse at this stage, as you will risk getting tense. Be confident that it will all start to flow when you step up for real. Just remind yourself of the key words and the links.

If you are offered the chance of meeting the audience before your talk for, say, a cup of coffee, then take it. It will help you relax and give you the opportunity to start breaking down any barriers. Your ice breaker will do the rest.

The final thing you should do before actually going in front of your audience is to visualise the first and last minute of your talk. You will have learnt them word for word, and picturing yourself saying them will give you confidence. It will help settle any nerves.

You are now more than ready for your speaking engagement.

Lessons Learned

'There are always three speeches, for every one you actually gave. The one you practiced, the one you gave, and the one you wish you gave.' Dale Carnegie

Soldiers will almost certainly have what they call a 'wash-up' after every operation. Its sole intention is to identify the lessons they learned so that they can work out how to rectify next time what went wrong.

If you get the chance to mix with your audience afterwards, they will be the best source for your lessons.

In a tactful way, ask them to tell you what you just told them. It's a good litmus test to see if you got your messages across.

If you can't meet your audience, ask the organiser of the event how he or she found your talk. Tell them you are not a sensitive person and you just want to improve your public speaking.

Whatever happens, take some time, yourself, to run over how your speech went. Did you miss anything out? Did the audience take in what you were saying? If not, why not? Do you need to alter your script in any way, if you are going to give the speech elsewhere? Did your jokes go down well?

Be self-critical. It's the best way to improve.

PART III

ORATORY AIDE-MEMOIRE

Introduction

We now return to the science associated with public speaking –
the processes described in Part I.

Some time ago, as I was trying to find a simple way of going
through the hoops to prepare for a speech, I put together my
own method.

I share it with you now and, although it is a formula, it does not
have to be completely prescriptive. It is up to you to imbue it
with your own way of doing things.

That said, if you are new to public speaking, I recommend that
you use this methodology to help you get underway. After all,
it's unique.

You may find that you stick with it, if only because it is based
on many years of experience.

I hope it will soon be developed into an app, so that it can be
used on your phone, tablet or laptop.

The basis of it is three spreadsheets. The first is designed to
help you do the analysis, the second to help you structure your
speech well and the last to allow you to produce your speech
notes – your aide-memoire.

It is, therefore, your guide and route plan as you progress
through the steps to your destination.

As you get more practice at giving speeches, you will find that
you can speed through the processes, such that you can put
together some speaking notes for a speech with remarkable
ease.

For now, just try it out in one of your own exercises and see
how it can help you.

Analysis

You will recall that, during the analysis, you are trying scientifically to think through your speech. It's the equivalent of a brainstorming exercise.

In essence, you ask yourself a series of questions, in a fixed order, about which you then ask yourself 'so what?'.

Your answers lead you to make conclusions on what you are going to speak about and in what order.

They also help you work out what sort of tone you need to adopt and what, if any, visual or other aids you might use.

The analysis spreadsheet (overleaf), on which you write the answers to your questions, can obviously be amended by you to suit your particular needs.

You may wish to add other questions and can, of course, increase the size of each cell as you write in your answers. Get it to work best for you.

The 'So What?' column is the important one when it comes to putting together your options and your eventual plan – the structure of your talk. So, make sure that your answers are tailored to do just that.

I have included the row numbers and column letters to assist you in your layout. Although, this spreadsheet is not linked to the other two and can just as easily be on a Word or Pages document. I have simply put it on a spreadsheet so that it can be on the same Excel or Numbers file as the others.

	A	B	C	D
1		**QUESTION**	**ANSWER**	**SO WHAT?**
2				
3	**PURPOSE**	WHY AM I GIVING THIS SPEECH?	To...	
4				
5	**TIMINGS**	WHAT TIME OF DAY IS MY TALK?		
6		AM I THE FIRST OR LAST SPEAKER?		
7		AM I ON JUST BEFORE A MEAL?		
8		AM I ON JUST AFTER A MEAL?		
9		HOW LONG IS MY TALK?		
10		HOW MUCH TIME WILL I LEAVE FOR QUESTIONS?		
11		HOW MUCH SPEAKING TIME REMAINS?		
12				
13	**VENUE**	DOES THE AUDITORIUM HAVE A STAGE/LECTERN?		
14		HOW LARGE IS THE AUDITORIUM?		
15		IS THE AUDITORIUM WELL LIT?		
16		DOES THE AUITORIUM HAVE A SOUND SYSTEM?		
17		WHAT ARE THE ACOUSTICS LIKE?		
18		DOES THE AUDITORIUM SUPPORT POWERPOINT ETC.?		
19				
20	**AUDIENCE**	HOW MANY IN THE AUDIENCE?		
21		HOW DIVERSE IS THE AUDIENCE?		
22		WHAT AGE IS THE AUDIENCE?		
23		ARE THEY LIKELY TO BE ON MY SIDE?		
24		WHAT SORT OF IMPRESSION DO I WANT TO MAKE?		
25		WHAT SORT OF MOOD DO I WANT TO CREATE?		
26				
27	**MESSAGES**	WHAT IS MY MAIN MESSAGE 1?		
28		WHAT ARE THE SUB/SUPPORTING MESSAGES TO 1?		
29				
30				
31		WHAT IS MY MAIN MESSAGE 2?		
32		WHAT ARE THE SUB/SUPPORTING MESSAGES TO 2?		
33				
34				
35		WHAT IS MY MAIN MESSAGE 3?		
36		WHAT ARE THE SUB/SUPPORTING MESSAGES TO 3?		
37				
38				
39				
40	**HUMOUR**	WHICH OF MY JOKES WILL SUIT THIS AUDIENCE/TALK?		
41				
42	**QUOTES**	WHICH QUOTES WILL SUPPORT THIS TALK?		
43		WHICH QUOTES WILL THIS AUDIENCE RELATE TO?		
44				
45	**STATISTICS**	WHICH STATISTICS SUPPORT MY MESSAGES?		

Analysis

Structure

The next spreadsheet (overleaf) has the structure of your speech on it, in accordance with your scheme of manoeuvre, which was discussed in Chapter 3.

Again, I have included the row numbers and column letters to assist you in your layout. It's important that you keep to the designated columns, as the three key words in Column D will appear in your aide-memoire automatically. You will see this shortly.

Clearly, if you decide on a different plan, then you can alter the spreadsheet accordingly.

The cells in Column C will need to expand greatly, as this is where you start to construct and write your script. You can do this by formatting the cell and, under 'Alignment' making sure you 'Wrap text'.

If you set the print area for this column only, you will get the entire script when you print.

Later, as you cut your script down to your outline, you can print it off again.

Selecting the three key words to go in Column D is of huge importance. These will become your speaking notes or your crib sheet, so you will need to make sure they are absolutely pertinent and memorable.

	A	B	C	D
1	STAGE	QUESTION	ANSWER	ABBREVIATED (3 WORDS)
2				
3	PURPOSE	WHY AM I GIVING MY SPEECH?	To...	
4				
5		WHAT IS MY ICE BREAKER?		
6	BEGINNING	WHAT IS MY HOOK?		
7		WHAT IS MY TALK ABOUT (OUTLINE)?		
8				
9		WHAT IS MY MAIN MESSAGE 1?		
10	MAIN MESSAGE 1	WHAT IS SUB POINT 1/1?		
11		WHAT IS SUB POINT 1/2?		
12		WHAT IS SUB POINT 1/3?		
13				
14		WHAT IS MY MAIN MESSAGE 2?		
15	MAIN MESSAGE 2	WHAT IS SUB POINT 2/1?		
16		WHAT IS SUB POINT 2/2?		
17		WHAT IS SUB POINT 2/3?		
18				
19		WHAT IS MY MAIN MESSAGE 3?		
20	MAIN MESSAGE 3	WHAT IS SUB POINT 3/1?		
21		WHAT IS SUB POINT 3/2?		
22		WHAT IS SUB POINT 3/3?		
23				
24		WHAT IS MY SHORT SUMMARY?		
25	END	WHAT IS MY FINAL JOKE/QUOTE?		
26		WHAT IS MY CALL TO ACTION?		

Structure

Aide-Memoire

The final spreadsheet (overleaf), your aide-memoire, is linked to the Structure spreadsheet, so needs to be on the same file.

Aide-memoire comes from the French word meaning literally 'a memory aid'. So, it's important that you have more or less committed your speech to memory. Otherwise, the key words on the aide-memoire will be of little use. They are there to jog your memory.

Again, I have included the row numbers and column letters to assist you in your layout. It's important that you keep to the columns, as the key words from Column D of your Structure spreadsheet will appear in your aide-memoire automatically. You can see this in rows 2, 4, 7, 9 and 11.

You may wish to use a colour system to differentiate between the parts of your speech. Indeed, you can embellish it in any way you choose, to help make the words more memorable.

If you find it easier to remember images, rather than key words and links, you could adjust the layout and include pictures or emojis as reminders.

When you have used it a few times and are completely at ease with the layout, you will be able to remove the headings. This will save you space and make your crib sheet even smaller.

Finally, you can print it out at whatever size suits your needs, including your eyesight. You may wish to use an especially large font, so that you can see it at a distance on, say, the lectern, as you move around. Alternatively, like me, you can print it on a C6 envelope, as it fits in a jacket inside pocket. The choice is yours.

	A	B	C	D	E	F	G	H	I
1					PURPOSE				
2					=QUESTIONS!E4				
3			MAIN MESSAGE 1		MAIN MESSAGE 2		MAIN MESSAGE 3		
4			=QUESTIONS!E10		=QUESTIONS!E15		=QUESTIONS!E20		
5	BEGINNING								END
6	ICE BREAKER		SUB POINT 1/1		SUB POINT 2/1		SUB POINT 3/1		QUICK SUMMARY
7	=QUESTIONS!E6		=QUESTIONS!E11		=QUESTIONS!E16		=QUESTIONS!E21		=QUESTIONS!E25
8	HOOK		SUB POINT 1/2		SUB POINT 2/2		SUB POINT 3/2		JOKE/QUOTE
9	=QUESTIONS!E7		=QUESTIONS!E12		=QUESTIONS!E17		=QUESTIONS!E22		=QUESTIONS!E26
10	ABOUT TALK		SUB POINT 1/3		SUB POINT 2/3		SUB POINT 3/3		CALL TO ACTION
11	=QUESTIONS!E8		=QUESTIONS!E13		=QUESTIONS!E18		=QUESTIONS!E23		=QUESTIONS!E27

Aide-Memoire

CONCLUSION

Public speaking is an art; a performing art. The speaker has to craft his or her speech creatively and deliver it with passion, sincerity and conviction.

But, it is also a science, as there is a process to go through if the speech is to be a success. There are few shortcuts, and none for the novice.

We have covered the steps you need to tread to analyse and put together the structure of a speech. These are the building blocks for success.

But, speeches don't give themselves, so we have talked through the manner in which you should approach the sometimes-daunting prospect of actually speaking publicly.

Using stories to get messages across is fundamental. Although, your style and manner are what will make you stand out.

Almost as important is the method you select to convey your words, such that they are easily understood, convincing and memorable.

Practicing enough to imbed the speech in the memory is crucial. That, combined with notes produced from the aide-memoire, will guarantee a great speech.

Good luck!

Notes